The Dragon

crack

Written by Roger Carr
Illustrated by Scott Vanden Bosch

Mario saw something big and white in the long grass under the tree.

"What a big egg," he said. "I'm going to take it home and see if Mom knows what kind of egg it is."

On the way home,
something in the egg went BUMP!

"What was that?" said Mario.

Something in the egg went BUMP!
again.

"What can it be?" he said.
"I hope Mom knows what it is."

Mario took the giant egg home.
"Mom, look at what I found," he said.
"It is very heavy, and I think
there is something moving inside."

"It looks like a dragon egg,"
Mom said.
"Let's put it in a blanket to keep it warm
and wait to see what happens."

The next morning, Mario jumped out of bed. He ran to see what had happened to the egg.

"WOW! Look Mom! Come and see! It really is a dragon!" Mario said.

"What do dragons eat?" Mario asked.

"Why, pasta, of course," Mom said.

Soon the dragon grew bigger.
Mario took care of it and fed it.
He played with it in the yard.

The dragon grew bigger and bigger.
It was too big to fit in the kitchen,
so Mario fed it outside.

The dragon helped with the cooking.
The neighbors watched.
No one had ever seen a dragon
cook before.

The dragon got so big
that it scared some people.

"That dragon has to go," they said.

"No! It's my friend," cried Mario.

The dragon grew bigger and bigger and bigger.

One day some people came with a giant net, but they could not catch the dragon.

Mario and his mom were worried.
"What will we do, Mom?" Mario asked.

"I think it's time for your dragon
to leave," Mom said.
"Its wings have grown. It wants to fly.
I think it wants to go."

But Mario was sad.
He did not want his dragon to go.

"I've heard of a place where other dragons live," Mom said.
"Your dragon will go there."

The dragon spread its wings.

"It's flying! It's flying!" cried Mario.

The dragon circled the house,
and then flew away.

Mario looked sad.

"Don't worry, Mario," said Mom.
"Your dragon will be happier with the
other dragons."

"I know," said Mario,
"but I sure will miss him."
Then Mario remembered all the fun
he had with his dragon, and smiled.